BRITAIN'S
WARTIME
MILKMEN

BRITAIN'S WARTIME MILKMEN

Tom Phelps

CHAPLIN BOOKS

Copyright © Tom Phelps
First published in 2015 by Chaplin Books

ISBN 978-1-909183-68-1

A CIP catalogue record for this book is available from
The British Library

Design by Michael Walsh at The Better Book Company

Printed by Imprint Digital

Chaplin Books
1 Eliza Place
Gosport PO12 4UN
Tel: 023 9252 9020
www.chaplinbooks.co.uk

CONTENTS

Frontispiece: William Fryer was born in Lewes, Sussex and started work on his father's farm when he was eight. Soon he was working for his brother delivering milk by yoke and pail. When twelve he was working for a dairyman in Tunbridge Wells, again delivering by yoke and pail. At the age of twenty-five he emigrated to Massachusetts but returned five years later to resume duties as a milkman. He was still working as a seventy-one-year-old milkman at the outbreak of the Great War

The Teddington Dairy, owned by the Roberts family,
photographed in the early 1900s

1

PRELUDE TO CONFLICT

In the period before the Great War, most people in Britain would have been familiar with the phrase 'the cow with the iron tail'. It was mockingly used to describe how water pumps had been constantly misused by unscrupulous milkmen to water down milk deliveries. With wages low and working hours long, milkmen tended to value their jobs according to the opportunities they provided for profiteering, by giving short measure or by overcharging. These gains were cheekily referred to as 'sparrows'. Milkmen often toiled in excess of 12 hours a day for probably less than 28 shillings for a seven-day week and with no holidays, each serving around 100 customers and usually making three deliveries a day.

Legislation (The Food Adulteration Act of 1870) and a general rising of standards meant that by Edwardian times the population was enjoying a much higher standard of milk.

Although some milk was sold in bottles, most was sold 'loose': it was unpasteurised and conveyed on three-wheeled carts known as milk prams, which milkman pushed by hand. The 'pram' held a churn and the milkman would decant two gallons at a time into a hand can, which he carried to the customer's door. He then measured out the quantity the customer wanted, using a special dipper to fill the customer's jug or dairy can. Later visits to the same households were made to collect the empty cans, or to deliver any extra milk. Some milkmen serving in hilly districts would have a horse-drawn cart to carry their churn.

There were still some milkmen who favoured the yoke and pail method of delivery whereby a yoke was carried on the shoulders with a large can – sometimes containing up to five gallons – suspended from each side, but they had become few in number by the Edwardian period.

Some more enterprising dairies were embracing new ideas and the early part of the century saw the introduction of pasteurisation and the bottling of milk. After a visit by a journalist from *The Lancet* to the premises of E J Walker's Dairy in Kensington, the magazine said on

19 November 1910 that: 'the ordinary price of milk is 4d a quart but fresh drawn milk from the stall-fed cows of Mr Walker delivered in sealed, sterilised glass bottles is 6d a quart though when it is a question of feeding infants the extra cost may be an economy'.

At that time, the idea of sealed bottles was sullenly opposed by those few milkmen who had benefitted by giving short measure from the churn or who had got into the habit of leaving the churn lid open when it was raining, for some divine intervention. Relieved of the task of measuring, the milkman was now able to deliver to more customers in the same period of time and so – to the benefit of the milk companies – the size of rounds could be increased.

Manor Farm Dairy of Highgate in London switched to bottled deliveries of pasteurised milk as early as 1906 following fact-finding visits to Canada and the United States by its owners, the Lane family. In Glasgow the St George Co-operative Society was pasteurising milk as early as 1904, being the first Co-op to do so, and the Coventry Co-operative Society was the first Co-op to be bottling milk by 1913.

A Coventry Co-operative milkman with an early horse-drawn float photographed during the Great War. The Coventry Society was the first co-operative society to introduce bottled, pasteurised milk in 1913
(Bob Malcolm collection)

One Hundred Elms Farm was adjacent to Harrow Public School. This tiled panel was painted by Minton artist F E Dean and was commissioned by Greenhill Dairies for their shop in Harrow. It was displayed there for more than 50 years and is now on display at the Victoria & Albert Museum in London. Many milkmen were employed on farms and expected to milk the cows before starting their rounds

Winston Churchill had the opportunity to see milkmen hard at work when he was at school at Harrow. Adjacent to the grounds was One Hundred Elms Farm, owned by the Greenhill family who had farmed in the area since the sixteenth century. By the beginning of the twentieth century, Greenhill's milkmen were operating milk rounds in the area and from a dairy shop at the corner of Greenhill Avenue and St Ann's Road, on land they had bought from bootmakers Thomas Lilley and William Skinner – who later found fame for their nationwide chain of shoe shops. Greenhill's subsequently sold their business to W & E Long Ltd and the farm itself was one of the many 'town farms' that disappeared before the Great War as precious land was acquired for housing.

Not all milkmen were male, of course. From Victorian times a number of women, known colloquially as 'Milk Kitties', were employed to deliver milk, but their numbers were to increase significantly when their male colleagues joined the armed services at the outbreak of war. Older women delivering milk were often referred to as 'Milk Biddies'.

Typical of the many small dairies was Avington Park Dairy in Southampton, which was managed by a Mr Horne. In April 1912 their

milkmen arrived at work to hear the devastating news that the *Titanic* had sunk on its maiden voyage. The dairy was situated in Oxford Street, less than two hundred yards from the main dock gate and nearby were a number of hotels where many of the ship's passengers had spent their last night on land. In the same street was The Grapes public house, the preferred drinking venue of White Star seamen. The little dairy's milkmen would have served all these establishments: records show that 1,500 gallons of fresh milk was loaded onto *Titanic* and supplemented by 600 gallons of tinned condensed milk.

In 1914 the docks at Southampton were to become vitally important in transporting troops and for ensuring the nation received its imports. The British Expeditionary Force marched through its gates in August 1914 and adopted the name 'Old Contemptibles', taken from a reference made about them by the Kaiser.

Some milkman had seen war before, of course. Mr J H Potter, a milkman working for the Village Dairy in Plumstead, near Woolwich, at 2/6d a week, was a veteran of the Boer War. One day, after milking the cows, he had made a delivery to the soldiers at Woolwich Barracks. This had inspired him to join the Army and he had served with the Royal Artillery in Africa, dealing with what he referred to as 'trouble with the Kaffirs and Zulus'. He had become a groom to a captain who befriended him and bought him out of the army, enabling him to return to his role of milkman, working for a Mr Dibbins. There was fundraising, too, for the Boer War's widows and orphans. Milkmen working for R Higgs and Sons in south London were asked to raise money and, although it is doubtful if any of the milkmen were Scottish, they dressed in tartan kilts and became known as 'Higgs Highlanders'. In 1910, they were in demand again, this time to help raise funds for King's College Hospital, and so, with the aid of a real regimental pipers' band, a march was organised and the volunteers returned with full collecting boxes: a sum of more than four figures was achieved.

Perhaps to avoid the drudgery of long hours and poor pay, many younger milkmen – inspired by the belief of Britain's supremacy – immediately volunteered for Kitchener's Army to give active service when war was declared in August 1914, mistakenly believing they would be 'home by Christmas'.

Opposite: This milkman working for the Darlington Creamery poses in front of the dairy shop. Note that milk is 1½d a quart and the small hand-bell that is rung to attract customers to bring out their jugs suggests he may not have had a specified round (Bob Malcolm collection)

Milk being handled at the railway station at the turn of the century. George Barham first brought milk to London by train and called his company Express Dairies in recognition of the express trains (Bob Malcolm collection)

Photographed in early 1914, this Friern Manor Dairy milkman adopts a Chaplinesque pose The milkman's role was a difficult one, having to push his cart along roads often with muddy tracks or with poor surfaces and many potholes

Tommy Cotching owned the farm at Hangar Lane, Ealing. The cows passing through the gate are heading towards what is today's North Circular Road. The large house in the background, called Hotspur Lodge, survives till this day. The photograph was taken shortly before the outbreak of The Great War

'London's safest milk' was the boast of Welford's. The milkman is busy in the early years of The Great War (Bob Malcolm collection)

Serving the Nation – Henry James Carter Willis

Henry Willis was born in Whitchurch, Buckinghamshire and came to London as a boy in November 1874 to assist on a barrow round for Baldwin's Dairy at 31 Kilburn High Road. His first job of the day was to milk 21 cows kept at nearby Manchester Terrace.

His milkman's uniform consisted of a white smock which extended below the knees and a flat-topped felt hat which, having a heavy brass plate in front, often tell off his head as he bent down to measure the milk from the hand can.

Baldwin's Dairy was eventually taken over by Robert Hornsby, trading as The West London Dairy Company, and now Henry's duties included collecting milk from the milk trains arriving at Paddington and Kings Cross stations. Although the work was hard, and the hours long, Henry enjoyed pushing his milk pram in the capital. He was doing three deliveries daily but on a Sunday would only have one, so once he'd fed the cows afterwards, he could go home relatively early. A few years later he was given the luxury of a horse-drawn vehicle for his round.

He was still working as a milkman when war was declared and in 1917 his firm joined the then new United Dairies. His day started at 4am and he considered himself lucky if he finished by 6pm. During a one-month period during the conflict, the dairy was so shorthanded that he did two complete rounds twice daily.

2

THE GREAT WAR

When war was declared on Germany on 4 August 1914, scores of young milkmen joined Kitchener's volunteer army, which initially consisted of nearly 500,000 men in the 18-30 age group. Many of the nation's younger milkmen lied about their age to ensure they were enrolled and – by virtue of their job – they made ideal servicemen. They were physically fit, alert, had good memories and plenty of stamina, having demonstrated that they were able to keep going to the end of a milk round no matter what obstacles they encountered. A recruiting sergeant recalled noticing a young, athletic milkman serving near Buckingham Palace. He hailed the young milkman and asked if he would like to serve the King. 'Certainly' was the immediate reply. 'How many pints would he like?'

By the start of the Great War some milkmen were delivering milk in bottles but most still pushed milk prams – hand-carts supporting a large churn that held usually 17 gallons. The milkman's role was a difficult one because he had to push his cart along muddy, poorly surfaced and potholed roads, often with deep ruts that froze in winter, and had to make three deliveries a day.

At this time there were hundreds of small milk companies, often operating from the yard behind a dairy shop which sold milk, butter, cream, eggs and other fresh food products. The large 'town farms' had mostly disappeared as they had been in areas earmarked for housing development. In London, for example, the giant Harrods department store was built in fashionable Kensington on the site of the cowsheds of E J Walker's Dairy. The dairy had kept 60 cows and it was said that the cows stood 'with their heads in Chelsea and their tails in Kensington'.

To alleviate the wartime manpower shortage, many dairies employed women, together with older men in their sixties and even seventies. Alfred Ashwell of Alleyn Farm Dairies in West Dulwich was one of these older milkmen – he worked through the Great War and was to

PERAMBULATORS.

Those made for this Company are carefully examined before being painted. All inferior Wood and that containing sap is rejected.

No. 1.—Wheels 24 inches in diameter, with Iron Rails, ordinary Axles, and made to carry 50-quart Churn ... ... £6 10s. 0d.

No. 2.—Same as above, but with Brass Rails, Patent Axles, 27-inch Wheels. To carry 50, 66, or 80-quart Churn £8 10 0

With Iron Rails 8 0 0

No. 3.—Brass Rails and Margin round Oval. Patent Axles, 30-inch Wheel. To carry 50, 66, or 80-quart Churn £10 0 0

With Iron Rails 9 10 0

No. 4.—Two-wheeler. Patent Axles, bold Side Boards, Brass Rails for Cans, 42-inch Wheels. To carry 66-quart Churn. These run easier than those with three wheels, and are much in vogue with the Express Country Milk Company, Limited £10 0 0.

Swing Box for carrying Butter, Eggs, and Books, extra 10s. 0d.

The above prices include Painting and Picking out, any colour, for No. 1, and with 60 1¼-inch Gold Letters for Nos. 2, 3, and 4. All are well Varnished and Finished in a workmanlike manner.

MUSEUM STREET, LONDON, W.C.

A page from a catalogue in the period just before the Great War showing that a new milk pram could be purchased for £10 or less

lose a son killed in action. Charles Bidmead Hatto was 53 when the war began and, in addition to his milk duties, he enlisted as a special constable in Kensington, being promoted to sergeant. The strain of holding down two jobs led to his ill health which meant that he retired when the war ended. Mrs M A Woodbury delivered milk in the Belgravia area and was over 50 when the conflict began. She had been working for Prett's Dairy and may have been the very last person still delivering with a yoke and pail in London. Her round was sold to Welford's in 1914 and she remained a milk woman throughout the war, but switched to using a milk pram.

Charles Bidmead Hatto in his special constable uniform

To keep deliveries going, a number of men unfit for military service were also recruited. One of these was 'Little Reggie' Mathews. Despite having a deformed foot he was said to be always smiling and cheery as he pushed his hand-cart through the streets of his round. Later he opened a shop 'Mathews, Footwear Specialist' in Larkhall Lane, Clapham.

Boys were recruited too, some as young as 14: a heavy responsibility to thrust onto young shoulders, but it is worth remembering that boys of this age were considered to be adults – indeed, they could legally marry until the law was changed in 1929.

In Highgate, the newly recruited women of Manor Farm Dairy found they were unable to push the large prams loaded up with bottles but, with typical ingenuity, they found a way around the problem by converting their prams into barrows that could be pulled by a donkey. Ben Davies & Son also used donkeys, which occasionally would wander out from the yard and into the nearby Chelsea police station. These donkeys were kept to provide asses' milk which was popular with some customers, from Victorian times through to the Great War.

Welford's Dairy was now operating the largest number of rounds in London. The business developed under Richard Welford who had taken over the business in 1859, at the age of 16, following the death of

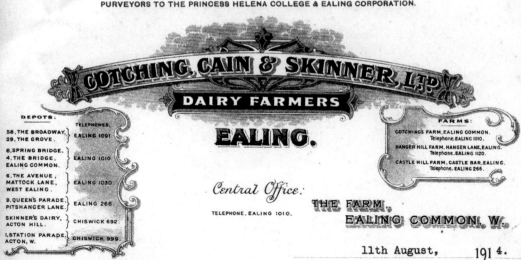

GOTCHING, CAIN & SKINNER, LTD.

DAIRY FARMERS

EALING.

DEPOTS:

58, THE BROADWAY,
29, THE GROVE.

TELEPHONES.
EALING 1091

8, SPRING BRIDGE.
4, THE BRIDGE,
EALING COMMON.

EALING 1010.

6, THE AVENUE,
MATTOCK LANE,
WEST EALING.

EALING 1030

9, QUEEN'S PARADE,
PITSHANGER LANE.

EALING 266.

SKINNER'S DAIRY,
ACTON HILL.

CHISWICK 692.

1, STATION PARADE,
ACTON, W.

CHISWICK 999.

FARMS:

GOTCHINGS FARM, EALING COMMON.
Telephone, EALING 1010.

HANGER HILL FARM, HANGER LANE, EALING.
Telephone, EALING 1120.

CASTLE HILL FARM, CASTLE BAR, EALING.
Telephone, EALING 266.

Central Office:

TELEPHONE, EALING 1010.

THE FARM,
EALING COMMON, W.

11th August,   191 4.

Dear Sir (or Madam),

  Owing to the entire change in trading conditions brought
about by the War, we find that to enable us to maintain our supplies
and service to our customers, and to prevent any undue rise in prices,
it is absolutely necessary for us to have a greatly increased cash
working capital at our disposal.

  We must therefore appeal to our customers to help us in
the present difficulties by paying up their current accounts with us
as closely as possible; by so doing not only granting us a real favour
but helping to prevent any rise in price.

  Whilst we are extremely sorry to trouble you, we venture,
in the above circumstances, to ask you to kindly let us have a
cheque on account at your earliest convenience.   The amount standing
to your debit on our books to Saturday last was £   .

  We beg to be allowed to take this opportunity of thanking
you for your esteemed patronage, and in anticipation of the kind
favour of your cheque.   Assuring you of every attention to your
wishes and that every effort will be made on our part to continue
rendering you an efficient service during the time of stress before us.

     Yours obediently,

*War was declared on 4 August 1914. Within a few days milkmen from this dairy were
delivering letters appealing to customers to pay their bills*

his father. He was later joined by his younger twin brothers. The Great War caused many business headaches for the family, because the fashionable houses of Belgravia were left deserted as the gentry stayed in the country. As Richard stated: 'The only residents were the caretaker and a cat'. Milk sales, however, stayed steady because many military hospitals needed huge supplies.

Many of the far-reaching changes in the lives of milkmen, made in response to the Great War, became permanent. It had been usual for most milkmen to make three deliveries a day to their customers,

This young milkman with his handcart was photographed during The Great War. He worked for Vale Farm Dairy in Sudbury between Wembley and Harrow. The dairy could not survive the strain of the Second World War and was purchased by United Dairies in 1942. Vale Farm is now a popular sports centre with playing fields

but now deliveries were mostly reduced to twice daily. The midday delivery, known as the 'pudding round', was discontinued but this did not lighten the load of the milkmen, because many were required to operate the many vacant rounds as well – the common practice was for two men to cover three rounds. The customers, however, were no doubt grateful: a nation at war often had to bear grim news with thousands of fatalities, missing soldiers and devastating reports of reverses in battle, but all this could be more easily digested with that very British tradition – a cup of tea.

The army's requirement for men, horses and vehicles made it impossible for dairies to continue to compete with each other. The Government was forced to commandeer horses and vehicles and in many

Milk arriving at a busy railway station from the West Country during the Great War

cases this meant that 90 percent of the male employees were recruited for the armed forces. These problems were overcome by wartime agreements whereby milkmen distributed milk in greatly reduced fleets of vehicles and exchanged customers to minimise the distances travelled. The strain on the milkmen was enormous: as well as doing two rounds a day and perhaps working for a new employer, serving newly transferred customers and dealing with shortages of supply, they had to deliver letters telling customers about all the changes. Luckily, milkmen could explain many of these changes during their afternoon round, which was when they usually met their customers.

The new zoning agreements soon became formalised and by the end of the war many new partnerships had been formed, which would benefit from less competition, bigger rounds, fewer vehicles and more effective use of manpower. This unity of purpose led to the formation of United Dairies, which came into being as the companies realised it was important to 'unite' during hostilities. The inspiration behind United Dairies was Sir William Price, who saw it as a way for London to receive its milk despite the difficulties of the war. He had moved to the capital from Llantwrtyd in Wales and, with his wife, had begun a retail milk business, later known as the Great Western and Metropolitan Dairies. After the start of the Great War, with not enough milk available, he contacted small producers all over the country and arranged for them to supply London for the first time. In this difficult period, he would start his day by telephoning from his bedside at 6am and would often continue working until 11 o'clock at night.

Milkmen working for larger companies, such as Long & Pocock, Curtiss Bros & Dumbrill, Aylesbury Dairy Co, Welford & Sons, Ben Davies & Son, Eastern Counties Dairy Farmers, The London Gloucester and North Hants Dairies, and the wonderfully named Crumpled Horn Dairy, all

COTCHING, CAIN & SKINNER.

THE FARM,
EALING COMMON, W.
February 6th, 1915.

Dear Sir or Madam,

We respectfully beg to intimate that the price of Milk will be advanced

ONE HALFPENNY PER QUART

from **Sunday, February 7th.** We much regret that this step should prove essential after the strenuous efforts and considerable financial sacrifices which we have made to avoid any change in the price of Milk.

The shortage of labour both on the farm and in town, the high price of feeding stuffs, and other difficulties experienced both in the production and delivery of Milk make this course necessary.

We feel that when you consider these circumstances you will see that the rise in price is inevitable, and we confidently appeal to you for a continuance of your kind support.

Assuring you of our careful attention to your orders and respectfully thanking you for your kind patronage.

Yours faithfully,

COTCHING, CAIN & SKINNER.

Outrage! Milk is increased by a farthing a pint in February 1915

found themselves working for the newly created United Dairies. These new larger companies were known as 'combines'. Many firms could see the benefits of the amalgamation and, despite being initially very suspicious of the new alliance, they wanted relief from their wartime problems, so, in the latter years of the Great War, they too joined United Dairies, though for a decade continued to use their old trading names.

Not everyone was convinced, however, and some smaller independent companies made a virtue out of not being part of a combine. The Express Dairy had been founded by George Barham in

Miss Nellie Gamble was in the milk trade for a total of 43 years. She started work as a milkwoman in January 1916 at the age of 18

Colonel Arthur Barham, one of the founders of United Dairies, who was unable to persuade his older brother Titus to bring the Express Dairy into the new organisation

1864. He is reputed to have brought the first milk into London by train – from Penshurst in Kent – and had named the new company the Express in recognition of the very fast locomotives used. The outbreak of war curtailed their fiftieth anniversary celebrations: although they were a relatively small company, they had 163 employees on active service – many were to be killed or be so seriously injured that they could not return to the physically demanding job of milkman. The Express, which was then being run by Titus Barham, a shrewd businessman, was invited to join United Dairies along with The Dairy Supply Company, owned by his younger brother Arthur. Although Arthur was keen to join, Titus steadfastly refused. This caused a rift in the family that would last for many decades, with milkmen working for the blue of Express and their rivals for the red of United Dairies.

The first board of United Dairies was drawn from the boards of its constituent companies, with the exception of its chairman, the Earl of Suffolk, who was elected but never presided over any meeting, being killed in action in France in 1917. He was replaced by Sir Reginald Butler from Wiltshire.

Throughout Britain milkmen worked mostly for small family businesses and this meant that when sons and husbands joined the armed services, it was impossible for some dairies to carry on. As a consequence many ceased to exist and were taken over by rivals, meaning that any milkmen still retained were working for a new employer. In Winchester, milkmen working for the long-established Collis Dairy joined forces in 1918 with their previous rivals to form the Collis, Cobb & Spencer Dairy, operating from opposite the historic Hyde Abbey. In West London, Mr Johnson, of Hangar Farm Dairy, decided to sell his business to Tommy Cotching and – to ensure customers would not migrate to a milkman from another company – sent out letters to customers strongly recommending the new firm. Afterwards, the same milkman would deliver another letter from the new owner welcoming the customer and assuring him that service and milk would still be of the

ECONOMY
DURING
WAR and Peace.

A pamphlet on "The best foods to buy during the war"—"The highest nutritive value at the lowest cost," issued by the "Medical Officer" newspaper, and distributed by many Medical Officers throughout the country, contains the following:—

"Fresh Milk is a remarkable food, as it contains every necessary kind of food substance."

The remarkable economy of pure new Milk is best indicated by a simple statement of the amount of various foods required to equal the food value of one quart of Milk, as proved by the highest scientific authorities.

ONE QUART OF PURE MILK EQUALS IN FOOD VALUE ANY OF THE FOLLOWING:

s.	d.		
1	0	worth of	RUMP STEAK.
1	6	„	EGGS.
2	0	„	CODFISH.
3	0	„	CHICKEN.

YOU SAVE MONEY BY USING MORE MILK!

A "basin of Bread and Milk" is the Cheapest and Most Nourishing meal obtainable.

A leaflet from the Great War informs customers of the value of milk, especially a bowl of 'bread & milk'. Another leaflet to be delivered by the overworked milkmen

The shortage of manpower may be the reason this Dunn of Upton Park pram has two churns. Rounds had to be bigger and perhaps this is why two churns were used. It certainly would have been an effort to push two full churns

highest quality. This practice still continues a century later.

Many milkmen worked for dairies that remained independent, among them Kirby & West of Leicester, Clifford's Dairy of Hounslow and Job's Dairy based in Surrey – all founded in Victorian times. They, along with the many Co-operative Societies rounds throughout the country, maintained a

Dairies were desperately short of staff. A 1915 newspaper advertisement appeals for new staff emphasising that the rounds are easy

high level of service. Handel Job had worked for Louisa Roberts and her husband Edward and, after he married the widowed Louisa in 1901, he gave his name to the firm that was to trade independently and be run by the Roberts family for the next eight decades, and through both World Wars. Job's also had a profitable bakery business and were able to acquire many local bakeries owned by people of German origin who found that their business failed because the public would not patronise a German firm. (The strong anti-German feeling when hostilities began meant, incidentally, that milkmen working for Kirby and West found

A delivery of milk arrives at St Mark's, Chelsea during the Great War in 1914. The milkman is C Heath of LWD. Many hospitals received huge quantities of milk because of the large number of casualties

Alfred 'Daddy' Ashwell was over 60 when war broke out. He is pictured in his summer straw boater and there is a churn cover over the milk churn to keep the milk cool

that Hanover Street in Leicester, where their premises was located, had been renamed Andover Street.)

Louisa Job's sister was Sally Prewitt, whose husband James owned Prewitt's Dairy and her great friends were Arthur Culver and his wife, who traded in Surbiton. On dismal wartime mornings, Mrs Culver would meet the milk train at Kingston station and enlist the help of any willing soldiers to lift heavy churns onto her horse and cart, because the porters demanded a shilling to lift the churns. Later, Culver's Dairy and Prewitt's Dairy were taken over by Job's.

There were also vendors who did not have established rounds but walked the streets shouting 'Milko!' while selling cut-price milk from their handcarts. To announce they had arrived they would noisily bang their churn with a lump of wood or ring a hand-bell. One such man was Mr Handsley, who operated in Streatham, south London, but with only ad hoc customers, these vendors could not exchange customers with other dairies when hostilities broke out and, with the loss of manpower to the Armed Forces, their businesses failed.

In January 1918 food shortages, caused mainly by the German sinking of ships, meant that the Government was forced to implement rationing for the first time. The price of milk increased dramatically from 4d a quart to 7d a quart; and butter, a dairy best-seller, was being replaced by margarine, which was much cheaper.

In October 1918, with the war almost over, Higgs Dairy decided to raise money for the Red Cross in London. Lids of quart milk-cans were soldered closed with a slot cut for coins. Virtually all dairies in London backed the campaign and there was an overwhelming response; on 29 November 1918, just after peace was declared, James Higgs handed over a cheque for the then staggering amount of £12,747.1s.0d. to the Lord Mayor.

Many servicemen returned from the War to resume their jobs as milkmen. While in service, J Lane, a milkman in Maida Vale, had been with the British Red Cross attached to the RAMC and in early 1915 he was sent to a hospital in France where he was required to move bodies from the operating theatres to the mortuary. Milkman A Townsend, from Fulham, joined the Royal Marines in 1914 and served in *HMS Botha*. He was transferred to the armed merchant ship *Seralia*, a 21,000 ton cargo ship and on 15 September 1918 he was torpedoed. Eighteen of the 27 crew were drowned but the enemy submarine that had torpedoed his ship then surfaced and the commander helped the survivors to retrieve their life raft and wished them good luck. Eventually, after 16 hours, they were picked up by a collier and taken back to Fishguard. Many of the lads, however, who had left their rounds to fight for King and Country were destined never to return to the role of a milkman: one of the many casualties was Private Frederick Kay of the Royal Fusiliers who had been a milkman for three years working for Cotching, Cain & Skinner in Ealing. When news of his death reached his mother, two of her other sons had already been injured in the conflict.

Ben Davis, a founding director of United Dairies, reflected on the difficulties of the Great War in a speech recalling 'scarcity and restriction, ration cards and food queues ... when horses left their stable in the morning the next feed often was not in store ... A man joining up was not to be replaced .... in a normal staff of 100, only eight of the older men were left to carry on with the aid of women and girls'.

The result was that many of the boys and women who had been recruited into the dairy trade during the war remained in their jobs after it ended.

Serving the Nation – Florence Taylor

One of the many women who delivered milk during the Great War was Florence Taylor who was born in 1894. She worked for the Aylesbury Dairy Company and was said to be the first milk girl in Putney High Street. This was in 1915 when women were asked to volunteer for various jobs. She pushed a milk pram and sold milk, cream, eggs and butter. Milk was 2d a pint, while skimmed milk was just a penny; half a pound of butter cost 10d and many customers bought as much as half a pint of cream daily. Wages were only 18 shillings a week but with a good commission this could rise to around £3. Weekly takings were usually just over £50.

After a few months she was given a horse and cart and asked to deliver in Wimbledon. At first she was very wary of horses, especially after she received a nasty kick, but she soon became very attached to her horse which always looked smart with the brass of the harness well polished. Florence started her day at 5am and usually returned to the dairy around 3.30 pm, after which she had the harness to clean and was also required to wash and scrub the 17-gallon churn and the hand-cans before going home.

During the War she delivered milk to soldiers quartered at Wimbledon and as she went past at six o'clock in the morning, she would give them an early call. Because of this the soldiers nicknamed her 'the Bos'un!'

Serving the Nation – Ray Rookes

Ray Rookes was a milkman during both World Wars, firstly as a young boy and then, during the later campaign, as a more mature man. Born in 1899, at the age of 14 he was recruited by local firm Long & Pocock of West Ealing to push a milk pram, filling one of the many vacancies caused by the departure of older men to serve in the armed forces. The firm had been founded in 1897 by Walter Pocock and his brother-in-law Walter Long, both Wiltshire men. Ray rose daily at 3.30am to begin the first of his three rounds. He was required to measure milk into customer's cans, charging them 4d a quart. He described many of his customers as pretty parlour maids.

Long & Pocock had been the first in the area to introduce three daily deliveries and this had been a major contributor in gaining new customers at the beginning of the century, but staff shortages meant that they had to abandon the midday 'pudding round'. Kitchener's volunteer army recruited men between the ages of 18 and 30, although the upper age limit was later raised to 40. Ray eventually joined the Royal Fusiliers before the conflict ended and he served in France. He retired in 1964 after 50 years' service as a milkman and it was estimated that in his career as a milkman he had walked 150,000 miles, the equivalent of six times around the world.

3

PEACE FOR OUR TIME

This was the first 'bottle' round to be introduced in South London in 1926.

The period after the Great War saw major changes in the role of the milkman. Britain's allies in Canada and the USA were more advanced in pasteurising and bottling techniques and visits to these countries ensured the British dairy industry soon became acquainted with more modern ideas and techniques. Although bottled milk had been available in Britain for more than three decades, used especially for infants, it was now seen as the way forward across the industry. At first, milk bottles had cardboard discs inserted into the mouth of the bottle to form a seal, but the mid-30s saw the emergence of new, slender-necked bottles with a more hygienic aluminium foil cap. This cap covered the outside lip of the bottle so dust could not gather. The cardboard tops

"HYGEIA"
BOTTLE
DISCS

The SAFE HYGIENIC SEAL for use with every kind of Disc Milk Bottle. "Hygeia" Discs are Safe, Sterile, Serviceable, both sides and edges well waxed

SOME EXAMPLES OF
SPECIALLY PRINTED DESIGNS

Any design printed to order. Suggestions and quotations for special designs submitted on request. Packed in cardboard tubes, each containing 500 Discs

PRICES PER THOUSAND

Quantity			Specially printed in one colour with or without Press Centre	Quantity			Specially printed in one colour with or without Press Centre
25,000	...	...	1/6	250,000	...	...	1/1½
50,000	...	...	1/3½	500,000	...	...	1/0½
100,000	...	...	1/2½	One million	...	...	11½d.

NOTE.—Smaller size "Hygeia" Bottle Discs (34 millimetres) can also be supplied at same prices as listed above.

TWO-COLOUR PRINTING—The extra cost for Two-Colour Printing is as follows :

3d. per 1000 extra on all orders under ¼ million.
2d. per 1000 extra on all orders of ¼ million and up to ½ million.
1d. per 1000 extra on all orders of ½ million and upwards.

DEFERRED DELIVERIES—Orders for any less quantity than ½ million to be delivered in one consignment.

Orders for ½ million can be delivered in two consignments spread over, but not exceeding, six months.

Orders for one million can be delivered in four consignments spread over, but not exceeding, twelve months.

NOTE.—25,000 is the minimum quantity in which SPECIAL DESIGNS can be printed.
Carriage Paid on 50,000 and upwards.

See next page for additional Bottle Disc designs and prices.

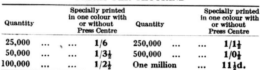
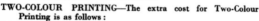

Showrooms:- MUSEUM S⸠ᵗ. LONDON. W.C.1. Branches:- EDINBURGH. BELFAST & LIMERICK.

Bottles had cardboard discs inserted into the neck. Collecting these discs was a favourite pastime of 1930s children. There was a variety of designs and a popular game for children was 'pogs' using bottle-tops

had been popular with children, who used them to play a game called 'pogs', but the slender-necked bottles gave the illusion of more cream at the top of the bottle – and housewives were soon in favour! Obliging milkmen placed empty cream pots over these foil-capped bottles to protect them from the birds, which learned to peck through the tops to drink the cream.

A London Co-operative Society handcart with metal crates to carry bottles. Roofs to handcarts were introduced in the late 1920s and said to be the idea of former milkman George Maycock who lived to be over 100

The advent of pasteurised milk did not entirely eliminate the popularity of sterilised milk, a product introduced in the Victorian era and often used to take on board ships because of its long-life qualities. It continued to be popular in Birmingham and many northern towns and, indeed, its taste was preferred to fresh milk when used for making custard and rice puddings.

The growing pace of change meant there needed to be large, efficient processing factories for bottling and this meant that vast quantities of milk needed to be moved from farms to processing plants and then to new distribution depots. Glass-lined, petrol-driven road tankers were first used from 1924 and then in December 1927, Sir William Price of United Dairies organised the first glass-lined rail tankers, which would eventually replace railway churns. These travelled to London from Calveley in Cheshire and Wootton Bassett in Wiltshire. On board for the inaugural trip was Sir William. Four tanks were coupled to ordinary passenger trains and uncoupled at Willesden Junction before being shunted to the new processing depot at Scrubs Lane, overlooking Wormwood Scrubs prison. One single tank replaced 300 railway churns and the emptying process was quicker and quieter.

Small dairies were merging as larger distribution depots were created, and some of these buildings were beautifully designed, such as the one at West Wickham, Kent, which opened in 1932. The industry's investment in bottles, distribution depots, horse-drawn floats, and new road and rail transport was considerable.

The introduction of milk bottles meant that dairies were able to increase the size of many rounds, as milkmen no longer had to measure out the customers' requirements: now there were 300 customers per round whereas previously it had been just 100. Handcarts needed to be redesigned too, to hold bottles (which in the early days had been held in wooden crates) – and it was soon realised that horse-drawn floats were necessary to carry the heavier loads on many rounds.

So began the golden era of the horse-drawn milk float. More milk could be carried and milkmen increased their range of dairy items with cream, eggs, butter and cheese, plus jams, tinned fruit, cereals and biscuits added to the stock. For most of the period the price of milk remained at 7d a quart.

Milkmen developed a love for their horses; the horse got to know its round and the places to stop and wait before moving on, as it kept pace with the milkman. This considerably reduced walking for the appreciative milkman, while feeding the milkman's horse was a favourite pastime for customers and children. Horses, being intelligent animals, got to know their routine and on the first round of the day would trot without stopping unless the milkman called out 'Whoa!' On the second round, when the milkman was knocking on doors to sell and talk to customers, they knew they must wait until commanded to move on. Many horses, however, would stubbornly refuse to go back out when they had completed their two daily rounds.

Horse-drawn floats were fitted with lamps that required filling with paraffin and had wicks that needed to be trimmed. As this was a messy job, many milkmen bought candles at their own expense to place in the lamps. In snow or icy conditions it was necessary to fit frost screws into the horseshoes. Concerned with the noise level of their early morning deliveries, dairies fitted their floats with rubber tyres and at least one company experimented with rubber horseshoes to quieten the horses' hooves, but this was abandoned as it caused lameness.

In 1927, during a visit to the new premises of Curtiss & Dumbrill in

Left top: Collecting in the rain for the 1928 Dr Barnardo's Appeal. These children give generously to help those in need

Left below: This housewife gives willingly to help the Dr. Barnardo's Appeal

Above: A B Mansfield's premises were near a Dr Barnardo's home and many of the children earned a few pennies by helping the local milkmen

Streatham by the Duke of York (the future King George VI), milkman Tom Parr, who loved horses, met the Royal party and jokingly offered to give the young Princess Elizabeth riding lessons.

Things were not all rosy, however. Until the Great War, fathers had been the principal breadwinners in a family, so their death or serious injury caused much poverty and, as a consequence, there were many destitute families and numerous children were taken into care homes. In 1928, dairy companies larger and small (and supported by the Co-operative Societies) held a 'Milk Week for Dr Barnardo's Bairns'. Posters went up in dairy shops and milkmen carried out house-to-house collections, using 18,000 specially designed collecting boxes, made in the shape of a quart-sized milk bottle with a handle and a slot for coins. The aim was to raise enough money to enable all boys and girls in Dr Barnardo Homes to be given an extra pint of milk each day for a whole year, which would amount to 100,000 gallons.

Advertising material in the late 1930s emphasised the importance of milk for the healthy development of children. This image appeared on posters, booklets and even milk vehicles

With unemployment levels staggeringly high by 1932, because of the Depression, United Dairies introduced a six-day week, giving milkmen a day's rest while recruiting additional staff to cover rounds. By the summer of 1932 unemployment in Britain had reached 3.5 million with many more only able to find part-time jobs. Having been recommended by his father, who was already a milkman, young Jimmy Gallant was taken on in the St John's Wood area and saw 50 years' service. Because the milkman's job was demanding, only high-calibre, fit young men were normally recruited. They were smartly dressed in uniforms often with military-style caps, believed to have been inspired by the soldiers' uniform of the Great War. One of these very fit young milkmen was Beaumont Asquith, a Co-op roundsman in Barnsley, who played football for the local team. He later joined Manchester United and, during the Second World War, made guest appearances for many clubs including Blackburn Rovers, Leeds United and Huddersfield Town. He once scored five goals in a match against Darlington.

Milkmen had to be adept with figures, too. Charles Redford was an Edinburgh milkman who emigrated to California and found similar employment there. Having an obvious ability with figures, he then changed career to become an accountant with an oil company during the Second World War. His son, born in California, became famous as the film star Robert Redford.

In the 1920s, poor prices for wheat and beef had forced more and more farmers into milk production: the result was considerable over-production and milk prices fell to un-remunerative levels. The answer was to increase consumption. In the 1930s successive governments produced two Agricultural Marketing Acts, the second of which paved the way for farmers to set up – in 1934 – The Milk Marketing Board, which took over the marketing of all the milk produced in England and Wales. The guaranteed market for milk was not good news for all producers, and indeed it was the death knell for many small dairies who relied on farmhouse pasteurisation. However, the Board's advertising campaigns did lead to an increase in milk drinking: by 1938, national consumption had risen by 42 million gallons a year, and by 1939 by another 40 million gallons. One of the propaganda tools used by the Ministry of Agriculture was that 50 percent fewer working days were lost by firms who supplied milk for their staff each morning, while the Milk Marketing Board aimed its advertising at children and housewives, much of it stressing the health benefits of milk to babies and young children.

The depot at West Wickham, Kent is a fine example of Milk Depot architecture and was opened in February 1932

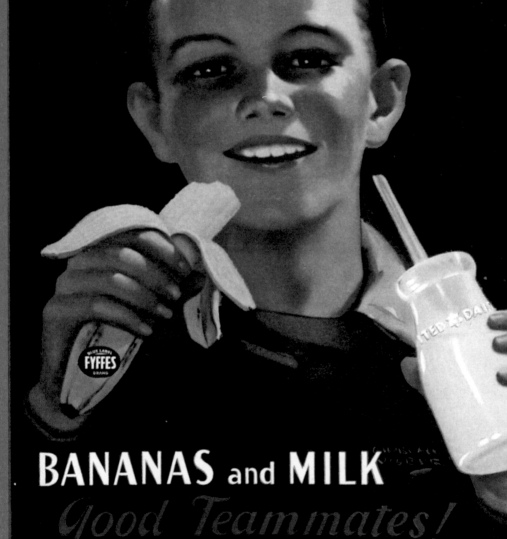

Advertising was skilfully aimed at children and products that need milk.
The UD Price list and magazine originated in the 1930s

Since the early 1930s, battery-powered electric milk floats had been making an appearance. Job's Dairy and many other small companies had quickly embraced the new delivery methods. There was no resistance from Job's milkmen because, like a number of other dairies, their deliveries were still being made by heavy handcarts rather than by horse-drawn vehicles. By the outbreak of the Second World War, there were many electric floats in operation. The Bristol Co-operative Society had 300 electric vehicles; Home Counties Dairies had 150, while Express Dairies had 100.

In London, United Dairies boasted that they now served every street in the capital and such a proclamation even appeared as advertisements on the sides of buses. The claim was slightly dubious, since that would have meant serving every street within a 14-mile radius of Trafalgar Square – no mean feat!

The milkman now featured widely in popular culture. In the 1920s G K Chesterton was writing the popular Father Brown novels and had his arch villain Flambeau steal milk cans to set up the mythical Tyrolean Dairy Company in London: the dairy had no cows and no milk, yet 1,000 customers. In 1936, in the film *The Milky Way*, comedian Harold Lloyd played Burleigh Sullivan, a weedy milkman for Sunflower Dairies who is mistakenly thought to have potential as a prize-fighter At the first screening at the famous Carlton Theatre, Haymarket, all the attendants dressed as milkmen. The idea was that of John Armstrong, advertising director of Paramount Theatres, who was awarded the Quigley Silver Plaque – America's highest award for showmanship. The Carlton was also the first cinema to open a milk bar, on 3 March 1936, selling 'delicious milk drinks of all kinds' to its patrons and it proved to be an overwhelming success. Milkmen even featured in music and a popular hit song of the 1930s on both sides of the Atlantic was *My Very Good Friend the Milkman*.

Neville Chamberlain famously returned from Munich in September 1938 declaring 'peace for our time' but within a year Britain was at war with Germany. Milkmen were already being enrolled into fire-fighting and first-aid. The two decades between the wars had seen the British milkman reach a point whereby the demanding job was well-respected. The dairy business had gone from selling 'loose milk' to a modern, hygienic industry employing reliable and smart personnel, but once again, milkmen would have to serve their country in the time of war.

Pictured just after the Great War, this milkman was photographed working for Kirby & West in Leicester. The firm was to ensure deliveries through the two wars and continues to give a vital service to the citizens of Leicester today

Alperton Park Dairy was a casualty of the war. It was taken over by the Express Dairy. The two new Murphy electric vehicles were photographed just before hostilities commenced. The milkmen drivers are Johnny Marsh and Alfie Knight. When they were demobbed neither wished to work for Express Dairies so joined rivals United Dairies. Alf's vehicle coincidentally has the registration APD 269, the initials of Alperton Park Dairy

The Silent Electric Vehicle is seen outside the premises of the manufacturer T H Lewis purchased by the Express Dairy Company in 1931. They originally made milk prams

The very first electric milk-float on trial with United Dairies and made by the Victor Company. The war curtailed the trials and it was not until 1947 that the 'electrification' process really got underway for UD

The handcart belonged to United Dairies which was formed during the Great War when competing dairies realised the needed to unite to ensure that milk could still be delivered to grateful customers. The company again ensured milk deliveries were received by customers during the Second World War

A three-wheel Murphy 'Servitor' owned by Stapleton's Dairy. The business was started in 1770 by the widow Stapleton and survived until the Second World War when it was absorbed into the Home Counties organisation

Serving the Nation – Ernest Briggs

Ernest Briggs remembered the milkmen and milkwomen who kept deliveries going during the Great War and, in 1928, he too became a milkman, joining the Royal Arsenal Co-operative Society, pushing one of their brightly painted red handcarts in the Ashen Grove area of Wimbledon. The Royal Arsenal Co-op took its name from the munitions works at Woolwich and was formed in 1868. Ernest was out on his round when his wife Ethel gave birth to their son Raymond in 1934.

After war was declared, Ernest volunteered to join the Auxiliary Fire Service fighting the many fires that occurred as a result of the air raids. He continued as a milkman for the Royal Arsenal and was one of a team of milkmen who ensured that the housewives of Wimbledon got milk for their wartime cuppa, though hostilities meant that the Wimbledon Tennis Tournament was not held from 1940 to 1945. He built his own air-raid shelter in his garden and his house suffered some bomb damage, but Ernest soon patched things up, though his front garden railings were commandeered for the war effort. Raymond, meanwhile, was one of the many children evacuated from London and was sent to Gillingham in Dorset.

Soon after the war Ernest was given a brand new electric milk float painted in the Royal Arsenal's bright red livery. After nearly 20 years of pushing a handcart, he was enthusiastic about the new float. In 1965 he retired after 37 years as a Co-operative Society milkman. His son Raymond was to become a popular and innovative author-illustrator with many books to his credit, including *The Snowman* and *Ethel & Ernest*, the latter the telling the moving and funny story of his parents' lives.

4

THE SECOND WORLD WAR

At the time of the outbreak of war, the milk industry employed some 70,200 workers including milkmen, clerks, yardmen and managers. United Dairies had 1,000 men called up in the first week, while Express Dairies had more than 2,800 men eventually leave for active service. Again it was the womenfolk, young boys and older men who kept the doorstep service going. Some women took over their husband's rounds after they had been called up for duty. Often two women were employed to do the extremely arduous work of a large milk round. There were product shortages too: in January 1940, the rationing of dairy products was introduced and the milkman, often considered a friend of the family, would help customers to write up the names in their ration books. Blackout regulations also had an immediate impact, making it necessary to reorganise from two deliveries a day to just one during the hours of daylight.

Households were given a choice of two milkmen by the Government, one independent, and one from a Co-operative Society, to reduce competition and make more manpower available. Zoning agreements were formally written up, with copies issued to each dairy company in the area to ensure they all knew the regulations and where their milkmen could serve. As had happened in the Great War, the manpower shortage meant many milk companies did not survive and many were forced to merge or be taken over by larger enterprises.

Alperton Park Dairies, serving in the Wembley area, was taken over by Express Dairies, although the owner, Viv Ferris, was a cousin to Leslie Ferris, a high-ranking director with United Dairies. Zoning dictated that Alperton must go to Express territory while nearby Vale Farm Dairies was taken over by United Dairies as it was in a different zone. In 1944 Express bought the Chatsworth Dairy Company of Sheffield and The Manorcroft Dairy at Dewsbury, two more companies that found it impossible to continue independently. Trading in the Winchester and Southampton area were two long-established milk companies, Arthur Brown Ltd and Harrison's Model Dairies, but wartime difficulties meant that the companies merged in 1940 and rounds staff found themselves working for the newly named Brown & Harrison's.

One of many young boys who became milkmen was 14-year-old Lenny Edwards who started work on 9 February 1942 with a glowing reference from his headmaster. No driving licence was needed for a horse-drawn milk float, unlike motorised vehicles, but because he was underage, his father had to act as guarantor in case there were any cash irregularities. His starting wage was 19/6d a week and his first horse was aptly named 'Spitfire'. Lenny was asked to serve the village of Harmondsworth in Middlesex where, in 1944, the Air Ministry bought land near to the village to build an airfield, enabling the RAF to embark upon long-haul flights to Japan: the war ended before major work had started but, in 1946, the site became Heathrow Airport.

One other boy milkman was a lad called Sean Connery who was fourteen when, in 1944, he joined the St Cuthbert's Co-operative Society in Edinburgh: he remained a milkman until his acting career finally took off in the 1950s.

At Pinner in Middlesex, young United Dairies milkman Eric Avery, being only 16 in 1940, was one of a trio of workers who stayed overnight in the depot to look after the horses during fire-watch duties. During the night several bombs fell in the area and in the morning light he discovered one that was unexploded in the middle of the yard. Such a dangerous situation did not disrupt supplies, however: the resourceful milkmen simply sourced their milk from the nearby Harrow Depot and deliveries carried on as usual. Eric later married Daphne Walesby who worked in the depot office. She too had to take her turn on fire-watch duty and recalled having to sleep on a camp bed, terrified of the rats that scuttled around the stables in the darkness.

In nearby Uxbridge, Yvonne Stagg, another 16-year-old at the beginning of the war, who worked in the office at the Express Depot, recalled:

> Whatever happened – bombs, air raids, et cetera – we
> carried on. It was quite an adventure really. They took milk
> down to the Underground stations, and delivered it to the
> houses that had been bombed. People hadn't got windows
> or doors sometimes but they had their milk. I went home
> to lunch one day and I'd lived a couple of miles away from

the dairy office, and a rocket came down very close to it. Luckily, everybody was at lunch, but when I came back, it put me on guard, and I spent an entire afternoon sitting on the desk, surrounded by broken glass, while everybody went home to clear up their houses.

We shall not be beaten. Two milkwomen brave the elements to ensure milk is delivered whatever the weather

Despite the bombing, milk was regularly delivered and not infrequently delivered to the front of houses that had been completely demolished, in the knowledge that neighbours would know if the occupants were alive and would take the milk to them. Bombing of railways often meant that milk trains failed to get through and many processing and distribution depots were hit. Bombing devastation was everywhere, but nevertheless, a by-law relating to broken glass on highways or public places stated:

Any person placing, depositing, or leaving any article of glass, or any broken glass or sharp substance not being road materials, on any highway or public place, shall on summary conviction forfeit and pay a sum not exceeding forty shillings. Will persons responsible for the custody and return of milk bottles please take care that these articles are placed in positions that they are not liable to become broken and lie about to the danger of the public. They must not be left on the highway or in any public place.

To release labour, milk rounds were rationalised and measures taken to cover the rounds of dairymen whose premises had been blitzed. By the start of 1940 at least 700,000 children and mothers had been evacuated to the countryside and milk sales fell as much as 38 percent, while in some cities, rounds were merged. This reduction meant horses became surplus and were sold to the Army. Although milk rounds became depleted in the cities, consumption became much higher in those rural districts.

The Emergency War Budget introduced by Sir John Simon included the rationing of petrol, which had an effect on moving milk from processing plants to distribution depots, but few milkmen used petrol vehicles. Sir John also increased sugar duty, which led to higher prices for sweetened milk in tin cans.

Rationing of foodstuffs, introduced in January 1940, included dairy favourites such as butter and cheese. By March that year bacon, sugar and meat were also rationed, followed by tea in July. In 1941 jam, cheese, canned food and other goods were added. The introduction of the National Milk Scheme gave an undertaking to deliver milk to every 'priority household' where expectant mothers, children and invalids were allowed a pint a day. The rest of the population normally received two pints a week per person, although that was not guaranteed. By March 1945 the weekly ration had increased to two-and-a-half pints.

The yearly manufacturing output of milk bottles was 122,000,000, requiring 70,000 tons of glass, but *The Milk Industry* magazine reported that the wartime loss of milk bottles was running at 30 million per annum caused mainly by non-return by customers, although many bottles were destroyed in bombing raids. A campaign was launched to get customers to 'rinse and return' to help the war effort. As was the case with many dairies, Gordon Clifford, who was in charge of the family business started by his grandfather in 1874, had to ask his milkmen to return to can deliveries when glass became scarce.

Prior to the war, there had been widespread misuse of churns, milk crates and bottles by people to whom they did not belong. These illegal practices became so widespread that, in 1930, a firm called Milk Vessel Recovery Ltd was formed. Following the outbreak of war, the firm repeatedly appealed to the Ministry of Food to introduce an Order under the Emergency Regulations to make it an offence to wilfully use bottles that were the property of others. Under the 26 February 1942 Emergency Powers Order No 298, it was possible to prosecute people under the Merchandise Marks Act, the penalty for a first offence being a fine of £80 or imprisonment for four months.

It wasn't just glass that was a problem: aluminium was a precious commodity needed for aircraft construction, but some 2,270 tons of aluminium a year was being used to make foil milk-bottle tops. Rigid controls were introduced, supplies for milk-bottle capping were only obtained with great difficulty and experiments with other materials such as zinc, zinc-with-tin, and lead-based caps were carried out, but these were ill-fitting, easily came away when being handled, and could cause health problems. The answer lay in recycling. After an appeal to return aluminium foil caps from milk bottles for conversion into war material, *The Milk Industry* magazine reported that 80,000,000 had been handed to milkmen in the first few months. Many milk floats carried posters reading 'Aluminium bottle caps. Please return to us.' This was extra work for the milkman but they cheerfully collected the bottle tops from their customers and entered into friendly rivalry as to who could collect the most. It was not until 1942 that aluminium was once again released for bottle-capping. The efforts of the nation and especially the milkmen in recycling aluminium meant that the idea of Joan Curran of the Telecommunications Research Establishment of using floods of aluminium strips to give false echoes to German radar was able to be implemented.

Milk bottle caps bore slogans such as 'raw material is war material'. The Ministry of Aircraft Production urged housewives to hand in everything made of aluminium including 'cooking utensils of all kinds, bodies and tubes of vacuum cleaners, ornaments and even thimbles'. The response was overwhelming and had the morale-boosting effect of involving a large section of the public in the war effort. Wally Vivian and John Wright of United Dairies, with their horse Daisy, were two of the milkmen who would go out on Sunday afternoons and collect metal for the cause in the Bexley area.

In 1941 paper consumption was cut to 22.5 percent of its pre-war total. In January 1942 the United Dairies house magazine was therefore

A lorry-load of milk is being despatched to a nearby Army Camp by Kirby & West in Leicestershire

drastically reduced in size and number of pages, but this pocket-size version was welcomed by milkmen serving in the armed forces because it fitted into uniform pockets and, with its news of their former colleagues, was a comforting link with their peacetime jobs.

By October 1942, 90 percent of the world's rubber production had been lost and there was a shortage of motor-car tyres. The enterprising owner of Wren Davis Dairy, which had a motorised fleet serving in the remote and rural parts of Buckinghamshire, had his milkmen fit motor-bike tyres to their vans. At that time, with severe shortages of raw materials, United Dairies instructed staff to save everything. The directive even included notes on how to sharpen a pencil just to put a point on it, and, if using a sharpening machine, not to grind the pencil unnecessarily.

On advice from the government, instructions were issued to owners of horses about what to do during bombing raids. Horses were to be unhitched from their milk floats and tethered to lamp-posts or some similar object to avoid them bolting and, if nothing practicable was available, the horse was to be tethered to the rear of the milk-float. Only when this task was carried out, was the milkman to think of his own personal safety and take refuge. These might have been the instructions, but in reality no milkmen would ever leave his frightened companion, his faithful horse.

In 1940, milkman John Harber of Thornton Heath, Surrey, stayed with his horse when it slipped into a crater made by a bomb that had exploded behind his van. He held his horse's head and spoke reassuringly to her as further bombs fell. He was presented with a medal for bravery by Mr Robinson of 'Our Dumb Friends League'. The noise of bombing affected the horses badly, and volunteers would stay all night in depots to help keep them calm.

The weather was also often a problem during the war, with terrific snow blizzards hitting much of the country several times. There were rounds that on Monday 29 January 1940, in Berkshire and Buckinghamshire, were badly affected by the weather. At Yiewsley, just across the county border in Middlesex, two milkmen delivering by horse-drawn milk-float phoned their depot at about 4pm as they had still not finished their rounds in the affected areas. They arrived back at about 7.15 pm and, after a 15-minute break, set out again with a motorised vehicle, not returning until 10pm that night. The next day, to reach some outlying customers, it was decided to take one round at a time with two extra horses. With three horses pulling one van, they got through – the only vehicle to do so in this area – and their customers were naturally delighted.

The firm of C King, West Exe Dairy in Tiverton, Devon, had embraced new technology in the form of this Morrison 10cwt electric vehicle but a shortage of glass bottles and manpower saw this milkwoman delivering from a giant churn.(Keith Roberts collection)

Britain's milkmen were highly amused when there was a propaganda war with Germany over milk. The Milk Marketing Board issued a poster showing a soldier drinking a glass of milk with the slogan *'Now! Where's that bloke Hitler!'* It was reproduced in Voelkischer Beodachter, the principal Nazi newspaper, with the comment:

> *Germans. Tremble! The brave British defender – note the stupid face – has drunk a glass of milk. The Tommies seem to have drunk little milk so far, because in spite of careful search we have not been able to detect them anywhere in front of the Siegfried Line when according to their popular hit song – of Jewish composition – they wanted to 'hang out their washing!'*

When Dunkirk was evacuated in June 1940, the troops were landed on the Kentish coast and military trains were used to transfer them back to their barracks. In Guildford, the Women's Institute ladies were on hand to greet the troops by handing out sandwiches and cake as the trains stopped. The cry went out, however, for a cup of tea and soon the milkmen, office ladies and processing staff from Home Counties Dairies were there with churns of milk, making a brew for the men.

A friendly smile from the Clifford's milk lady delivering during the war

Every opportunity was taken to ridicule the Germans. Even the Milk Marketing Board joined in the 'fun' and decided to enter the cartoon propaganda with this wartime poster

While milkmen were doing their duties back in Britain, many were active in war zones. United Dairies sent Christmas parcels to company staff serving in the Armed Forces, containing a Christmas pudding, chocolate, playing cards, cigarettes and a copy of the staff magazine 'Our Notebook'.

Alfred Palmer who had been a milkman in Buckhurst Hill, Essex, became a naval reservist. Unfortunately he suffered severe burns at the Dunkirk evacuation and was sent to the Royal Naval Hospital at Chatham where his nurse was Miss E Gilbey, who had been his former bookkeeper at the depot.

E J Robertson, a milkman in Dulwich, had been a Territorial and was called up at the beginning of the war. His battalion entered Belgium during the early hours of 11 May 1940 to be met by thousands of refugees fleeing the other way. He recalled how three Hurricanes attacked a formation of 24 enemy bombers. Four Germans had parachuted out dressed as nuns, but they were rounded up and handed to the French, who immediately shot them. Then came news that the Allies were evacuating Belgium. He then fell back to a position 12 miles from Dunkirk and, after destroying all equipment so it would not fall into enemy hands, became part of the rearguard action. A magnificent reception of tea, cake and cigarettes met him and his colleagues at Dover.

On VE Day, Edward 'Lofty' Valance, a milkman at Edgware, became alarmed when the horse Snowball arrived back in the yard without his pal Harry Sutton. Edward feared some tragedy had struck but, as he was about to set off to look for Harry, he arrived on foot. Harry had been having celebratory cup of tea with his jubilant customers when Snowball decided to walk the rest of the round and returned to the depot alone.

Cowes Dairymen's Wartime Association.

The wartime zoning agreements between dairies was formalised into rule books so that no disputes should arise. This one covers the Cowes district on the Isle of Wight (David Pimm)

Most horses would obstinately refuse to go back out when their day was finished. The milkman would therefore need to use a bike to take items back on the round

A cheerful Jobs Dairy milkman with an electric handcart gets on with wartime deliveries

A Murphy electric milk-float delivered to Bluegates Farm Dairy, Ashwell in 1943

It's 1943 and the Buckinghamshire firm of Wren Davis take delivery of their first electric milk float. In the picture is Sydney Gough, their longest-serving employee at that time. Wren Davis Dairy still provides a service to the residents of Wendover and the surrounding area today (Keith Roberts collection)

Wally Vivian and John Wright would spend Sunday afternoons collecting pots and pans for the war effort in the Bexley area of Kent, accompanied by their horse Daisy. At this time all United Dairies milk floats carried an appeal to return aluminium bottle caps

These two women push a heavy handcart in 1943 to ensure that vital deliveries of milk get through to households. The indomitable British spirit!

The yard staff at the Burnt Ash Depot at Lee in Kent pose for their photograph when the processing lorry arrived very late due to wartime difficulties

With deliveries reduced to one daily, plus rounds being combined because of manpower shortages, the only way to get deliveries made was to load the milk-float to capacity and beyond

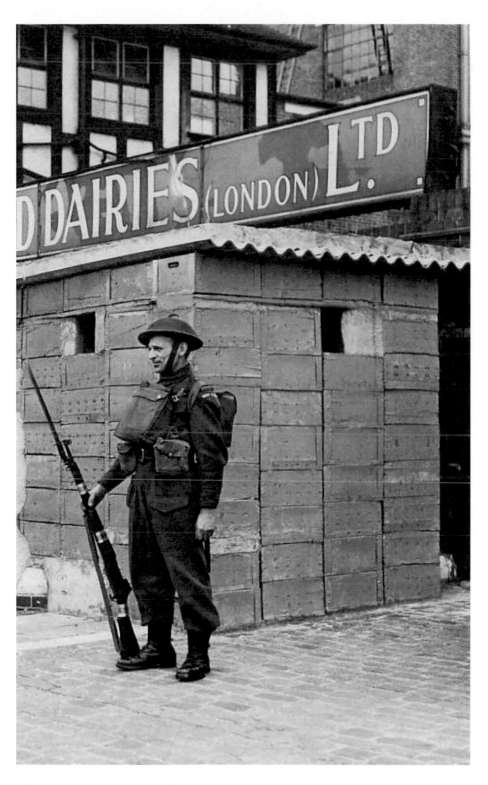

If the enemy arrives, they will not get any milk without a fight! Important installations had to be guarded including the Streatham milk depot

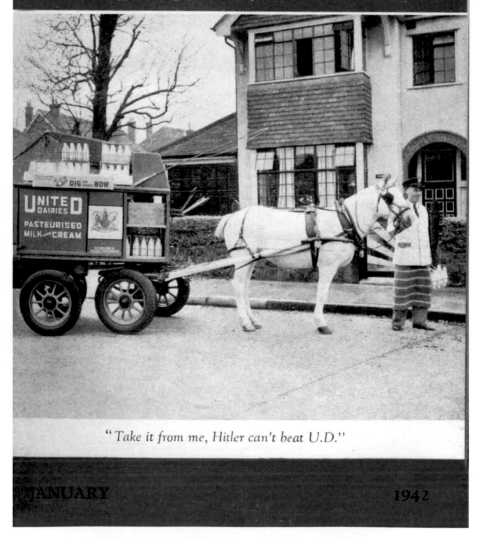

OUR
NOTEBOOK
The Staff Magazine of United Dairies

"Take it from me, Hitler can't beat U.D."

JANUARY   1942

The paper shortage resulted in the staff handbook, Our Notebook, being cut to pocket-size. This was the first edition in the new format with a typically strong message for Adolf Hitler

"MILKO! Sorry, only 'arf a pint again this morning, Madam!"

The cartoon demonstrates the grief milkman experienced from some outraged customers when milk was in even shorter supply

*With bomb damage all
around them, the milkmen
still had to obey this order*

*This cheerful milkwoman poses for a photograph with
her Job's Dairy hand cart*

*A customer stops this Express milkman to pay her
bill. Note the rubble left in the street from recent
bombing (Bob Malcolm collection)*

*A policeman informs that the air raid is
over. The young boy could actually be in
charge of the handcart
(Bob Malcolm collection)*

*Monty alights from the train at
Waterloo. Standing to attention
is L/Cpl F E Bourne who had
been a milkman from Finchley*

A newly painted milk float arrives at Yiewsley. Many floats were damaged by bombing

Wartime milk rounds were often amalgamated and considered too big for the volunteer ladies. Often two women would team up together to deliver the milk

Reg Hannam is pictured with his young son in 1942. Reg worked for Isle of Wight Creameries Ltd who used Shetland ponies to haul their milk floats (David Pimm)

This smartly dressed Clifford's milkman is making wartime deliveries in the Hounslow area

The scene of devastation at the Croydon Depot after a bombing raid on 1 and 2 October 1940. The depot finally closed in 1985 and now forms part of the Mayday Hospital complex

This 1943 cartoon highlighted the fact that milkmen had no trouble with early morning reveille

"It's a picnic! They let you lie in bed till 6 a.m!"

Two firms that could not survive the pressures of war were Harrison's Model Dairies and Arthur Brown Ltd, who both traded in the Southampton and Winchester areas. In 1940 they combined to form this new company but their milkmen still had to push these handcarts even though electric versions were available

By Appointment to H.M. King George VI

UNITED DAIRIES
WARTIME SERVICE

THE Pasteurised Bottled Milk Service maintained by the Company is yet another of those outstanding organisations brought into prominence by the War.

Through the difficult times of last autumn and winter, day and night the Service carried on. Many were the tributes paid by a grateful public to the Company's staff for "appearing as usual," as so many put it.

Hard blows have been taken and perhaps harder blows are to come. Whatever they may be, the Nation-wide organisation of United Dairies will be ready.

There is a Churchillian tone to this reassuring message from United Dairies

---

REGISTER NOW FOR
MILK
LAST DAY SATURDAY

In order to make the most of our winter supplies of liquid milk, and to ensure that those who need milk most will get it, EVERYONE must now register with the supplier of his choice. Saturday, August 23rd is the last day.

The scheme will give priority to the following:

(1) HOLDERS OF A CHILD'S RATION BOOK — one pint per day.
They must be registered even if they have a permit under the National Milk Scheme.

(2) EXPECTANT MOTHERS — one pint per day.
They must register even if they have a permit under the National Milk Scheme.

(3) HOLDERS OF A GENERAL RATION BOOK WHO ARE UNDER 18 AT THE END OF THIS YEAR — half-a-pint per day.
Like everyone else, they must register now.

(4) Special arrangements, which will be announced later, will be made for certain classes of INVALIDS, but they must register now.

Everybody who holds a ration book must register before August 23rd
EXCEPT
Permanent residents in hotels, boarding houses, and other establishments and children who will be back at Boarding Schools before October 1st, who must NOT register.

HOW TO REGISTER

[To economise in deliveries each household is advised to register with a single supplier, except in those cases where part of the household supply consists of certified T.T. or sterilised milk obtainable only from a second supplier.]

Use the spare counterfoil marked with a large ' C ' on page 25 of the general book (or page 23 of a child's book).

1. Write the holder's national registration number in the top right-hand corner of the counterfoil.

2. Fill in the holder's name and address and the name and address of the milk supplier.

3. Holders of general ration books who are under 18 at the end of this year (born on or after January 1st, 1924) must write clearly their date of birth in the bottom right-hand corner of the counterfoil. Holders of child's ration books need not do this.

4. Do not cut out the counterfoil. Hand the book to your supplier: he will cut it out.

5. Fill in the name and address of your milk supplier in the space marked ' spare C ' on the inside back cover.

DO IT AS SOON AS YOU CAN BEFORE SATURDAY, AUGUST 23rd.

Food Facts No. 55.   Issued by the Ministry of Food, London, W.1.

Bad News. Milk was to be rationed. The Ministry of Food urged people to register by newspaper adverts. For milkmen it was another major headache

---

This Express milkman poses for the camera wearing his white cap. Express milkmen looked forward to 1 May as it was 'white cap day' and the warmer weather was on its way. The practice was abandoned later in the War

*Looking somewhat lost, these evacuees drink their school milk,
thanks to the efforts of the local milkman*

*John Harber
pictured with his
beloved horse*

Utter devastation after a bomb fell on Leyton Depot on 15 September 1940. This did not prevent 'Stiffy' Williams and his pals from delivering to their grateful customers

A bomb fell outside the entrance to the Sutton Lane milk depot at Chiswick on 23 February 1944. The milk floats were unable to leave through the main entrance so with great enterprise they knocked down the fence to the left side of the depot and made sure all customers got a delivery

The United Dairies Price List and Magazine was delivered free by the milkman. It contained household tips, recipes, children's stories, film reviews and was much sought after

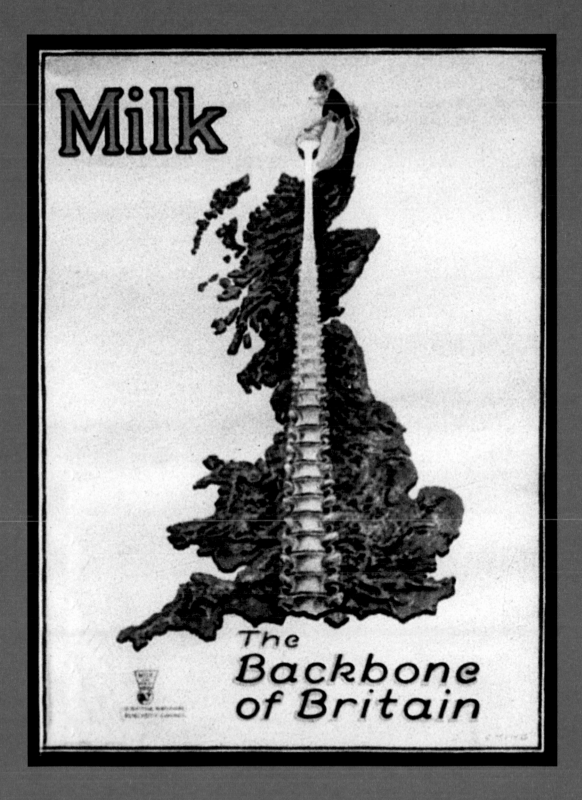

A wartime milk poster that surely would have the approval of Winston Churchill

Serving the Nation – Alfred Hawthorn Hill (aka Benny Hill)

Alfred ('Alfie') Hawthorn Hill was born in 1924 in an old Victorian house in what is now called Bernard Street, Southampton, barely 50 yards from the rear entrance of Avington Park Dairy. He attended Taunton's Grammar School in Southampton, leaving at the age of 16 after spending a few months as an evacuee in Bournemouth with his younger sister. In December 1940 when he was still 16, he joined James Hann & Son, trading as Dorset Dairies, as a milkman for a wage of just under £1 a week. At this time Hann's had 25 percent of their staff serving in HM Forces and a further 25 percent on standby. He was given a round that encompassed Eastleigh and the nearby village of Fair Oak. As he travelled back to Market Street in Eastleigh with his horse Daisy at a gallop, he imagined himself on a stagecoach riding into Dodge City. In addition to his milk round he had to groom Daisy, polish the brasses and apply dubbin to the leather harness.

He left Hann's Dairy in August 1941 to pursue his show-business career under the stage name of Benny Hill, but never forgot the enjoyable time he spent as a boy milkman during the war. Southampton was a major port and Eastleigh a key railway town and both were badly bombed. Alfie began his army career when called up in 1942. He joined the Royal Electrical and Mechanical Engineers and, as Craftsman Hill, saw action in Normandy three months after the main landing.

During his show-business career he devised a number of comedy sketches involving milkmen and in 1971 recorded the hit comedy record 'Ernie (The Fastest Milkman in the West)'. He remembered to include Market Street in the lyrics, a memory from his own days as a wartime milk boy. He also did a series of television advertisements dressed as a milkman for Unigate Dairies, the firm that now owned his wartime round.

Benny Hill pictured in 1971. He is in the studios advertising for Unigate Dairies

Benny Hill in 1971. Milkmen delivered loaves of bread as well as milk. Farmers Wife was a brand name that came from the Home Counties Dairy

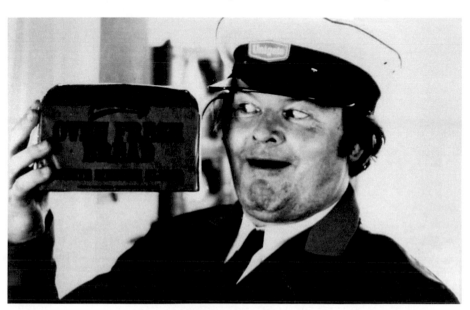

Serving the Nation – Albert Edward & Eliza May Williams

Albert Williams, known to his work pals as 'Stiffy', was called to active service on 18 September 1941. He served with the Eighth Army in Egypt, taking part in the Battle of Alamein, driving water tankers and ammunition lorries. Albert had joined United Dairies aged 30 at the Leyton Depot in east London and was an excellent salesman, winning a gold pocket-watch for his sales efforts in 1937. He made deliveries twice daily and, in addition to milk, a vast range of groceries was available to customers.

With the outbreak of war, deliveries were reduced to one each day during the hours of daylight and soon many of the grocery items were on ration. On 15 September 1940 the Leyton Depot was severely bombed but, despite the devastation, Albert and his workmates continued to deliver to their customers. Albert's round served the Trelawny Road E10 area and, with his horse Rita, he was a popular figure with his customers. When Albert was called up, there was such a shortage of staff that nobody could be found to take over and, to cover for her husband, Albert's wife Eliza May, known as 'Dolly', stepped into the breach.

Dolly was typical of those strong-willed women of the East End and she was to continue the Trelawny Road round with Rita until 1943, when an eventual replacement milkman was recruited. One Leyton colleague did not survive the war: J Harman was killed on active service. Albert was discharged from the Army through ill health in February 1944 and when he was fit enough, he returned to work for United Dairies. However, because of all the reorganisations there were no vacant rounds, so he went to the nearby Stratford Depot where he took on his new duties and from there he retired in the 1960s. Albert and Dolly obviously had a strong influence on their son Douglas, because he too went into the milk delivery business and had a very successful managerial career, retiring as manager of Haycroft Farm Depot in Harlesden where his wife Ann was head clerk.

Opposite page: Albert 'Stiffy' Williams of Leytonstone depot pictured with horse Rita in Trelawney Road E10 just before his call up at the age of 41
Above: Elizabeth 'Dolly' Williams of Leytonstone, seen here with horse Rita, took over her husband's round during the war. Her son Douglas used to help mum and he too became a milkman and went on to become a successful depot manager

5

COUNTING THE COST

When peace was finally declared with the surrender of the Japanese nation, it was hoped that things would soon return to normality. Britain's two biggest milk companies – Express Dairies and United Dairies – had suffered severe losses of men and property. United Dairies had lost 198 of its workers on active service with another 35 killed in bombing raids. Express Dairies reported that 118 men were lost in action. A tragedy occurred at Gap Road, Wimbledon when a direct hit on the depot killed four members of staff and 30 local residents who had taken refuge there.

Some 40 Express Dairies distribution depots were demolished or seriously damaged, while United Dairies had suffered bomb damage to 70 percent of their properties. Many of the smaller dairies, of course, had their premises wrecked. A massive outlay was in prospect: in addition to the war damage, there had been no wartime investment in new vehicles and much of the processing equipment was beyond its useful life. The result was that many smaller companies that had struggled to keep going though the war now were forced out of business. (Surprisingly, however, some things seemed indestructible: in the 1960s, when a bombed-out premises was being demolished, a crate of wartime sterilised milk was found – partly thanks of its long-life qualities, and the fact that the slimline bottles were sealed with a crown cork cap, it was still perfectly drinkable).

Meanwhile, servicemen were still needed in the occupied countries. Joseph Maggs, chairman of United Dairies, unsuccessfully pleaded with the government to release his 5,479 employees to enable milk rounds to work normally but, when they finally did come home, many decided that their future did not lie in the dairy industry. New skills had been learnt and new careers forged. With the demise of smaller dairies, and reorganisations due to bombings, many rounds no longer existed in their pre-war state, while war-wounded milkmen found a return to such an arduous job was now beyond their physical capabilities, causing a desperate shortage of staff. Many women and boys continued to operate their rounds.

A cartoon used by Alfred Slater & Sons of Birmingham
announcing the 'electrification' process

Returning milkmen often found they were given new rounds and many were annoyed that they were now offered a hand-cart round when – pre-war – they had had a horse-drawn float. Leslie 'Choc' Rowntree, formerly of Maida Vale, was so angry at such a change that he went to work in a rival depot. Choc's anger finally subsided and he later represented his company at cricket, football and darts.

The war had curtailed the introduction of battery-operated electric vehicles because many manufacturers had turned their factories over to the war effort. Moreover, the frequent power cuts in wartime for those that did already have electric floats meant vehicles often failed to complete their rounds and had to be towed back to the depot, often by an ever-reliable horse. However, in post-war Britain, electrification was still seen as the way forward. Dairies invested in new transport and many milkmen found themselves in charge of a brand new battery-driven vehicle. In the early 1940s Mr J A Priestley, a transport expert, had conducted experiments in Sheffield that showed that electric vehicles were faster than a horse over a ten-mile trip when stopping every ten yards. While this was correct for much delivery work such as parcels, coal merchants and brewery drays, it failed to recognise that on a milk round a well-trained horse could continue walking in the middle of the road, keeping pace with the milkman as he delivered from house to house.

Electric floats did not consume power while standing idle: with no internal combustion engine they made for easy maintenance and, having fewer parts, their working life was at least three times longer than a petrol vehicle. Although many dairy premises were cramped, 30 electric floats could be accommodated in a space previously occupied by 10 horses and vans, with all their bedding, manure and feedstuff. This enabled dairy companies to close smaller depots that were badly in need of refurbishment.

Soon, companies throughout Britain, including Cotteswold Dairies in Gloucestershire, Hanson & Sons of Liverpool, Cambrian United Dairies in Wales, Alfred Slater Ltd of Birmingham, and Edinburgh & Dumfriesshire Dairies were investing in electric vehicles. Not at all milkmen welcomed this, as they were losing their beloved horses, but others who had previously served their customers from hand carts were more enthusiastic. A legal loophole at the time meant that passing a test on a slow-moving electric vehicle – which had few controls – meant that milkmen were now entitled to drive a car if they wished, even if they had no idea how to do so.

The fleet of Morrison Electricar delivery vehicles outside the premises of G Cartwright & Sons, Dunstable Road, Luton in June 1946. The shop window pleads for bottles to be returned (Keith Roberts collection)

While some dairy companies ceased to exist, others grew massively. Gordon Clifford, who was operating a few rounds in the Hounslow area of West London, realised that there were opportunities and so expanded by buying a business in Sunningdale. He then further extended into Bracknell – which became a so-called 'new town' – and within a few

short years had built an empire that covered West London, Berkshire, Oxfordshire, Hampshire and Bristol. One of his wartime milk women had been Phyllis Long who eventually was promoted to chief buyer for Clifford's.

Winston Churchill, Britain's wartime Prime Minister, was defeated in the 1945 General Election and the new Labour Government embarked upon a programme of nationalisation. Among its many achievements was the inauguration of the National Health Service, but it had been Winston Churchill, giving an epoch-making broadcast on 21

The nation owed much to the efforts of the milkman in keeping spirits high during two world wars. To recognise their role, a fitting tribute could perhaps look like this

The days of horse-drawn milk floats were numbered after the War. The 'middle' design was the last type designed and built by United Dairies at Haycroft Farm. The milkman could easily step into these floats

Mrs Bennett making deliveries with daughter Val in 1946. Women continued as milk women because men were still in the Armed Forces

March 1943, who had spoken of the 'spacious domain of public health' and the need for establishing a National Health Service. In this same speech he endeared himself to the nation's milkmen by proclaiming: 'Here let me say that there is no finer investment for any community than putting milk into babies. Healthy citizens are the greatest asset any country can have.'

In this post-war period of austerity, a milk bottle shortage, together with continued rationing, made for more headaches for the milkman and it was 1954 before food rationing finally ended in Britain. However, in December 1946 there was good news for the milkmen of United Dairies when a decision was made to pay them a bonus of one week's wages in recognition of their efforts during the war.

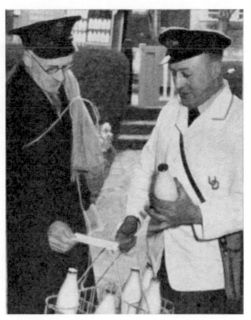

Getting back to normal. Milkman Jimmy Gallant meets up with the postman. Jimmy followed his father a milkman into the trade in the 1930s. He achieved 50 years' service broken only by the War. A younger, slimmer Jimmy was a good amateur boxer

Many brave milkmen who served in the Armed Services were destined not to return. John Scott became a milkman for the local Co-operative Society at the age of 14 after he left Usworth Intermediate School in County Durham. In 1943, when he was 18, he volunteered to join the RAF and became a flight engineer. In August 1944, with the rank of sergeant, he was posted to Waddington, Lincolnshire, where he was involved in many operations and was the only Englishman in an otherwise all-Australian crew. He died on 3 March 1945, just two weeks before his twentieth birthday when his Lancaster was shot down while he was on his twenty-first operation on a bombing raid over Dortmund.

James Conway was a young milkman from Stockport who became a Marine and was part of the team who, in December 1942, carried out the audacious raid on German shipping in the occupied port of Bordeaux. This was carried out in canoes and named Operation Frankton. Sadly, James along with nine others of the team, did not survive the mission, but its success was profound and Churchill reflected that it probably shortened the war by six months. This famous wartime operation was made into a film in 1955 – *The Cockleshell Heroes* – starring Trevor Howard.

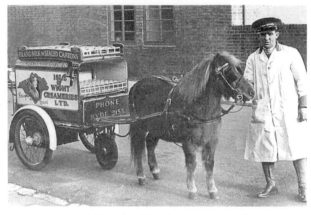

Customers of The Isle of Wight Creameries loved the Shetland ponies that the company used. The photograph was taken in Ryde in the late 1940s (David Pimm)

In addition to the personal tragedies, the two world wars had a direct effect on the role of the milkman – an effect that went beyond simply the passage of time and the introduction of new technologies. In essence the wars had forced the pace of change: what began the twentieth-century as a free-for-all with three deliveries, seven days a week, had – less than 50 years later – became one with just a single daily delivery and a choice between two competing milkmen, a practice that would continue for the next 50 years or more. In

With the war over, much military equipment became surplus. Jobs Dairy bought this 1946 ex-RAF six-wheeler to move milk from their processing factory at Hanworth to their milk depots in Surrey and Hampshire

74

With the day's work done, this Crown Dairies of Aberdeen 'Brush' milk-float returns to the milk depot

Wales & Edwards were a Shrewsbury based electric vehicle manufacturer who won the post-war contract to 'electrify' the fleet of United Dairies. This is a 'Standard' model

fact, it took technology a little time to catch up: for instance, although single daily deliveries had been introduced because of blackout restrictions and shortage of manpower, once the post-war austerity period came to an end, households were able to buy domestic refrigerators – so no longer needed more than one daily delivery of milk after all.

Britain's dedicated army of older milkmen, young boys and milk women had braved the bombing and wartime hardships even in the darkest hours and their role in maintaining the nation's morale was immeasurable.

Serving the Nation – Frank Staples

Born in 1923, Frank was an industrious lad who had a paper round, a Saturday job on a baker's round, and a Sunday job helping his milkman father for 6d. On one occasion his father was too ill to work and since young Frank knew the round, he was co-opted to help the relief milkman. So useful was Frank that the manager signed him up as a new recruit in 1938, aged fifteen. His first job was as a milk boy helping on a very large round in Bermondsey. In 1940, with the severe shortage of men caused by the need of the armed forces, Frank became a fully fledged milkman at the age of seventeen. He served the Kennington area near the Oval Cricket Ground in south London with his horse, Tony. On many occasions there were air raids but Frank would never leave his horse and, if the bombing was some distance away, they would carry on delivering. He found he was soon helping customers to read wartime leaflets and organise ration books. At the age of just 19, Frank was enlisted and his round passed to a woman. He joined The Royal Norfolk Regiment and, during the Normandy landings, was buried alive from a shell burst that shattered his eardrum. He was discharged from the army in November 1946 and returned to being a milkman, but was disappointed to be given a round with a handcart instead of a horse-drawn van. Milk was still being rationed and often there would be cuts of 10 percent or more and, while priority customers would receive their full ration, non-priority customers such as pensioners were left without supplies, which upset young Frank. During the severe winter of 1947 he found some old timber from a bomb-site and made a sledge so that he could drag 80 pints along in the snow. He married in 1948 and when his wife Gladys gave birth to a daughter, Amanda, in 1953, his appreciative customers gave him gifts of clothing for his new baby. In 1963 he embarked upon a successful managerial career and retired in the mid-80s from the milk depot at Thornton Heath.

Frank Staples and his horse Tony photographed near The Oval Cricket Ground

Acknowledgements

The author would like to thank Daphne Avery, Raymond Briggs (illustrator and author), Ben Davies Jnr, Amanda Field (Chaplin Books), Paul Gray (Birmingham and Midlands Museum of Transport), Paul Luke (editor of Milk Bottle News), Dave Marden (author), Simon Roberts (managing director of Job's Dairy), Frank Staples, Ted Webb (head of welfare at Unigate Dairies), Jayne Widdowson (of Kirby & West), and Doug Williams.

Photographs in the book are from the author's own collection, many of which were donated by the Welfare Department of Unigate Dairies in 2001. Other photographs were kindly supplied by Bob Malcolm, David Pimm and Keith Roberts (all as credited). Raymond Briggs provided the photograph of Ernest Briggs; Frank Staples provided the photograph of himself; and Doug Williams provided the photograph of his parents and the milkhorse, Rita.

A Milk Marketing Board poster that caused an angry response by the Germans
(see page 48)

Index